THE WEAPONS ENCYCLOPÆDIA

TANK AIRCRAFT AFV SHIP ARTILLERY VEHICLES SECRET WEAPON

HUNGARIAN TOLDI AND TURÁN TANKS

THE WEAPONS ENCYCLOPAEDIA

EDITORIAL STAFF

Luca Cristini, Paolo Crippa.

ACADEMIC EDITORIAL STAFF

Enrico Acerbi, Massimiliano Afiero, Aldo Antonicelli, Ruggero Calò, Luigi Carretta, Flavio Chistè, Anna Cristini, Carlo Cucut, Salvo Fagone, Enrico Finazzer, Björn Huber, Andrea Lombardi, Aymeric Lopez, Marco Lucchetti, Luigi Manes, Giovanni Maressi, Francesco Mattesini, Federico Peirani, Alberto Peruffo, Maurizio Raggi, Andrea Alberto Tallillo, Antonio Tallillo, Massimo Zorza.

PUBLISHED BY

Luca Cristini Editore (Soldiershop), via Orio, 35/4 - 24050 Zanica (BG) ITALY.

DISTRIBUTION BY

Soldiershop - www.soldiershop.com, Amazon, Ingram Spark, Berliner Zinnfigurem (D), LaFeltrinelli, Mondadori, Libera Editorial (Spain), Google book (eBook), Kobo, (eBoook), Apple Book (eBook).

CONTRIBUTORS OF THIS VOLUME & ACKNOWLEDGEMENTS

We would like to thank the main contributors to this issue: The profiles of the floats are all by the author. The colouring of the photos is by Anna Cristini. Special thanks to national and/or private institutions such as: Army General Staff, State Archives, Bundesarchiv, Nara, Library of Congress etc. To P.Crippa, A.Lopez, L.Manes, C.Cucut, Tallillo archives. Model Victoria (www.modelvictoria.it), for providing images or other items from their archives. For the realisation of this volume we also made use of AI systems.

For a complete list of Soldiershop titles, or for every information please contact us on our website: www.soldiershop.com or www.cristinieditore.com. E-mail: info@soldiershop.com. Keep up to date on Facebook & Twitter: https://www.facebook.com/soldiershop.publishing

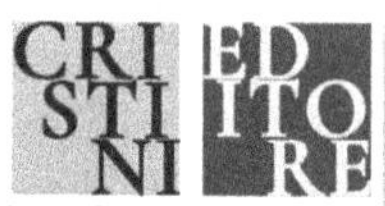

Title: **HUNGARIAN TANKS TOLDI &TURÁN** Code.: **TWE-013 EN**
Series by L. S. Cristini
ISBN code: 9791255890065 First edition July 2023
THE WEAPONS ENCYCLOPAEDIA (SOLDIERSHOP) is a trademark of Luca Cristini Editore

THE WEAPONS ENCYCLOPÆDIA

TANK AIRCRAFT AFV SHIP ARTILLERY VEHICLES SECRET WEAPON

HUNGARIAN TANKS TOLDI & TURÁN

LUCA STEFANO CRISTINI

BOOK SERIES FOR MODELERS & COLLECTORS

CONTENTS

▼ Toldi I tankn action during a test/training session at the Ludovika Military Academy in Budapest (see profile on Page 17). Hungary, 1942.

TOLDI LIGHT TANK

INTRODUCTION

The Hungarian light tank named 38M Toldi was developed on the basis of the Swedish Landsverk L-60 model and named after the 14th-century Hungarian knight, Miklós Toldi. After the V-4 prototype, developed at home in 1936, proved too expensive and work on it too slow, the Hungarian General Staff decided to obtain a modern light tank as soon as possible. Between April 1940 and December 1942, just under 200 examples of the Toldi light tank were produced locally by the Hungarian companies MA-VAG and Ganz. Despite having limited armoured protection and modest firepower, the Toldi represented Hungary's main armoured weapon until the end of 1941.

DEVELOPMENT AND DESIGN

After the First World War, the Treaty of Trianon in Versailles prohibited the Hungarian army (Honved) from developing and using tanks. Despite this, the Hungarians managed to purchase armoured vehicles from abroad. In the 1930s, the Hungarian army acquired over 100 *tankettes* (the well-known Italian L3 light tanks) for its armoured forces. However, these *tankettes* were already obsolete as combat vehicles, lacking an adequate turret, sufficient armoured protection and limited firepower with only two machine guns available.

▲ Toldi tank parade with its entire crew on 'display'. Note one of the many insignia used on Hungarian armoured vehicles (this particular flared cross can be seen in the profile on page 25).

▲ Column of 38m Toldi I tanks belonging to the 1st Transylvania Battalion in 1940. Author's colouring.

In 1936, the Hungarian army began to look for more modern tanks to supplement or replace the *tankettes,* while seeking superior firepower. For this purpose, they contacted several countries, including the aforementioned Italy, Germany and Sweden.

In the meantime, the Swedish company AB Landsverk had completed its recent design, the Landsverk L-60, in October 1937 and was looking for a buyer to cover at least part of the development costs. After a series of trials in 1937 with the V-4 prototype and the Panzer I, the Magyar heavy industries MÁVAG decided to purchase the licence of the Landsverk L-60 for further development.

Eventually, Hungary managed to acquire a single Swedish Landsverk L-60 light tank (with the serial number H-004) in 1937 (or 1936, depending on sources). There are several versions regarding the origin of the vehicle, some even indicating that it was directly built in Hungary.

After the arrival of the Swedish vehicle, test runs were conducted at home between mid-June and 1 July 1938 at the Haymasker and Varpalota test ranges. At the end of these tests, Hungarian General Garandy Novak, who was satisfied with the performance, preliminarily proposed the production of approximately 64 vehicles, intended for the two mechanised brigades and the two cavalry brigades. During these tests, the Hungarian V-4 prototype vehicle was also tested. After comparing the performance of the two vehicles, the V-4 was not adopted for service.

Subsequently, thanks to new and updated negotiations with Sweden, Hungary was granted a licence to produce the vehicle. At a meeting of the Hungarian War Ministry on 2 September 1938, it was decided to start production of the tank with some modifications, especially regarding armament.

Local companies MAVAG and Ganz then received an initial production order for 80 vehicles.

The Hungarian version of the vehicle was equipped with a local version of the Swiss Solothurn 20 mm anti-tank gun and a Gebauer 34/37.M coaxial machine gun. Due to the lack of Hungarian experience in tank production, the production process was delayed and the first batch of 80 Toldi tanks required the import of components from Sweden and Germany, including the Bussing-Nag engine.

The first Toldi tanks were completed in March 1940. Once the first series of 80 vehicles was completed, MAVAG was able to produce the necessary engine locally. After closely observing the rapid success achieved by the German armed forces during the western campaign in May 1940, the Hungarian army, like others, was greatly impressed and realised that the use of highly mobile motorised units was the future of modern warfare. Therefore, in anticipation of a future expansion of armoured forces, there was a demand for more Toldi tanks. Consequently, another order for 110 new vehicles was placed as

TOLDI I LIGHT TANK IN TRANSYLVANIA, SEPTEMBER 1940

▲ Toldi I of the 1st Hungarian cavalry brigade during the occupation of Transylvania, Romania. Note the insignia of the unit with the Turul bird with a sword in its talons (a kind of large hawk, a symbol of Hungarian culture). September 1940.

early as 1940. These second series vehicles were designated as Toldi II. Although some sources claim that the Toldi II was a more protected tank, this is not true. In fact, the only difference lay in the use of home-made components and some minor modifications to the suspension. With the exception of these details, the two types of vehicles were essentially identical.

▲ Detail of the Toldi's turret, with the cute mascot on board.

In order to speed up production, the transmission was built by Ganz and the rubber wheels by Ruggzantaarngyar. This made it possible to complete the second series of Toldi IIs using Hungarian-made parts, which was important since, due to the war, it was impossible to obtain additional parts from abroad. The Toldi II vehicles were marked with registration numbers ranging from H-281 to H-490. Mavag built the vehicles with registration numbers from H-381 to H-422, while Ganz built those with registration numbers from H-424 to H-490. The second production run lasted from May 1941 to December 1942, with a total of 202 units produced.

TECHNICAL FEATURES

The Toldi tank was developed to meet the needs of the Hungarian army in terms of mobility and combat in difficult terrain.

Hull and turret: the Toldi's hull had a standard layout with the transmission mounted at the front, the crew compartment or combat chamber in the centre and the engine compartment at the rear. Above the hull was an armoured superstructure that narrowed towards the engine compartment. At the front left of the vehicle was the fully protected driver's station, and the driver had an escape hatch at the top. For visibility of the surroundings, there was a front and a left side observation slot. On the front upper chassis, a headlamp was located inside a protected housing, with a grille door that could be lowered or closed as required.

The Toldi's turret had two crew hatches located on each side. In addition, there were two observation slits on each side without slits for visors. Finally, on the upper part of the turret was a command dome with a large one-piece hatch.

The dimensions of the vehicle vary slightly depending on the sources and also on the model. While most sources agree on a length of 4.75 metres, there can be differences in width and height. Depending on the sources, the width varies from 2.05 metres to 2.14 metres, while the height may vary from 1.87 metres to 2.14 metres. It is important to note that some sources may take the extended circular antenna into account for the overall height of the vehicle.

Armament: when the Toldi was introduced into the Hungarian army, the 20 mm 36M anti-tank gun was chosen as the main armament. The 20 mm 36M was essentially a licensed version of the Swiss Solothurn S 18-100 anti-tank gun (also mounted on some versions of the Italian L3 light tank). This choice was mainly motivated by logistical considerations, as the weapon was already produced locally under licence, ensuring an adequate supply of spare parts and ammunition. The 36M anti-tank gun had a rate of fire of between 15 and 20 rounds per minute. The armour penetration capability of the 36M anti-tank gun (at an angle of 60°) at a distance of 600 metres was, however, only 10 mm. Initially, the use of 3.7 or 4 cm cannon was briefly considered, but the adoption of such armaments would have required a restyling of the turret, so these certainly more suitable calibres were not included in the production.

As far as the ammunition load is concerned, sources vary. From a minimum of 52 rounds cited in *'Hungarian Armor, Wheels and Tracks'* by G. Finizio. Up to an allocation of 208 rounds cited in *'Axis Combat Vehicles'* by P. Chamberlain and C. Ellis. It is possible/probable that the low figure quoted of 52 rounds is

▲ A Toldi I crosses a street in the town of Villany in Hungary 1941. Author's colouring.

a typo and refers to the mounted gun of the Toldi IIa or Toldi III. As secondary armament, the Toldi was equipped with a Gebauer 34/37 8 mm machine gun. This could also be dismantled and used in an anti-aircraft function. Some 2,400 rounds of ammunition for this machine gun were carried inside the tank. As already mentioned, the last versions of the Toldi, starting with the Toldi IIa, had a 40 mm 36 cannon (and the long version on the Toldi III 40/43) with, in fact, about 50 rounds available.

Armour plating of the vehicle: the Toldi had limited armour protection. The front and side armour of the hull was only 13mm thick, while the upper, lower and rear armour was even thinner, only 6mm thick. The turret had a similar configuration, with the front and side armour 13 mm thick and the rear and upper armour only 6 mm thick. This armour was dangerously insufficient and could be easily penetrated even by Soviet anti-tank guns in use by the infantry at the time. The Toldi II retained the same armour, while the III saw it strengthened in some areas.

In an attempt to improve protection against such armaments, one of the vehicles (with the serial number H-423) was used to test the installation of side armoured skirts of German origin. Eventually this solution was adopted, although only a few Toldi received these armoured skirts. These lateral reinforcements were mainly used on the larger Turán tanks. As an example, see the profile pictures on page 27.

Engine: the Toldi was equipped with an eight-cylinder Büssing NAG L8V petrol engine of German origin, developing 160 hp at 2,200 rpm. The weight of the tank was around 8.5 tonnes (or 8.7 tonnes, depending on sources). Despite its weight, the Toldi was capable of a top speed of 50 km/h, which was considerable for the time. After all, the tank was developed to meet the requirements of the Hungarian army in terms of great mobility and combat in difficult terrain. However, this engine proved problematic for these vehicles and required constant maintenance and repair. To cope with this, starting in 1941, Hungarian manufacturers were able to start producing the engine locally, thus reducing dependence on imports.

The Toldi had a fuel tank with a capacity of 253 litres, giving it an operational range of around 220 km.

Suspension: Initially, no significant changes were made to the suspension and transmission construction compared to the Swedish Toldi model. The tank's suspension used a torsion bar system, which consisted of a front sprocket wheel, a rear idler wheel, four larger road wheels and two return rollers. However, although they did their job adequately, this suspension did not guarantee a particularly comfortable or smooth ride. It was known that the Toldi could be quite unstable during movement, especially over rough terrain. In the second Toldi series, some domestically produced suspension parts were introduced. Although

▲ A column of Toldi I belonging to the 1st Armoured Battalion. Author's colouring.

TOLDI I LIGHT TANK IN HUNGARY, 1940

▲ Toldi I of the 2nd Hungarian cavalry brigade. In this case the insignia is the typical Lorraine red cross. September 1940.

these parts were of slightly better quality than those originally used, they did not significantly change the overall performance of the suspension.

Crew members: the Toldi I and II had a crew of three. The crew arrangement was as follows:
Pilot: located at the front left of the hull, he was responsible for driving the vehicle. He had an escape hatch at the top of his driver's seat and could observe his surroundings through a front and a left side observation door;

Gunner/Gunner: located in the turret, to the left of the main gun, the gunner was responsible for operating the Gebauer 34/37 8 mm machine gun and loading the main gun;

Commander: also located in the turret, to the right of the gunner, the vehicle commander had several responsibilities. In addition to acting as radio operator (if the vehicle was equipped with radio equipment), the commander was also responsible for supervising the crew and making tactical decisions. He was also equipped with a command dome for better visibility of his surroundings.

Radio equipment: the Toldi Is used the R-5 radio, while the Toldi IIs were equipped with the more powerful R-5a radio. The Toldi I had a large round radio antenna mounted on the right side of the turret, which could be folded down if necessary. In the case of the Toldi II, the radio antenna was simpler and also mounted on the right side of the turret.

▲ A Toldi I crosses a street in a town in Transylvania. Author's colouring. At right above a Toldi tank in 1943

TOLDI I LIGHT TANK IN UKRAINE, 1941

▲ Toldi I of the 9th tank-cyclist battalion in the Ukraine in September 1941.

▲ View of the Hungarian Toldi I tankn front.

▲ View of the Hungarian Toldi tank from the rear.

VERSIONS OF THE VEHICLE

Three main versions were produced of the most popular light tank in the Hungarian army, with the exception of a few prototypes. It is important to note that the technical characteristics between the three main variants of the Toldi varied slightly, as minor modifications and improvements were made during the development and use of the vehicle. However, the information provided below represents the general specifications of the main versions of the Toldi tank employed during the Second World War.

Of the Toldi I also known as the A/20 we have already mentioned in the previous chapter. Its main feature was its weapon: the 20mm pseudo Solothorn turret-mounted cannon.

Toldi II, IIa and III: the Hungarians made several attempts to improve the firepower and protection of the Toldi tanks. The Toldi IIa version (also known as B20 the II and B/40 the IIa) represented a significant improvement over the previous models. It was finally equipped with a new 40-mm cannon, which offered more firepower than the 20-mm anti-tank gun mounted on previous models. In addition, the Toldi IIa featured thicker and stronger armour than previous models, at least in some critical areas of the vehicle, contributing to better crew protection.

Later, the Toldi III (also known as the C/40) was developed, which was similar to the Toldi IIa, but with even thicker 35 mm frontal armour. This further increase in armour thickness provided greater protection against enemy hits.

However, it is important to note that both of these upgrades, those carried out on the Toldi IIa and the Toldi III, were still not sufficient, and were in fact still inferior to the more heavily armoured enemy tanks. In spite of all the efforts made to upgrade the Toldi, the Hungarian tanks still remained light and relatively unprotected compared to the more advanced enemy tanks, and therefore not suitable for direct combat in a tank fighter role, for which, as we shall see below, an ad hoc option was devised!

▲ Toldi IIa with long 40mm cannon. Author's colouring.

The characteristics of the three main vehicles follow:

Toldi I:

- Weight: 8.3 tonnes
- Length: 4.55 metres
- Width: 2.06 metres
- Height: 1.85 metres
- Crew: 3 members (commander, pilot and gunner)
- Coring: 6-35 mm
- Main armament: 20 mm Solothurn S-18/100 cannon with 50 bullets
- Secondary armament: 7.92 mm Solothurn MG 34 machine gun with 2,000 bullets
- Engine: Manfred Weiss V-8 with 100 hp
- Maximum speed on the road: 43 km/h
- Autonomy: 200 kilometres
- Fording capacity: 0.8 metres
- Vertical obstacle clearance: 0.6 metres
- Total output: about 80 units

Toldi IIa:

- Weight: 9.5 tonnes
- Length: 4.72 metres
- Width: 2.06 metres
- Height: 1.85 metres
- Crew: 3 members (commander, pilot and gunner)
- Coring: 6-35 mm

▲ Toldi I of the 1st Armoured Brigade in the Ukraine (USSR) 1941.

TOLDI I LIGHT TANK IN HUNGARY, 1942

▲ Toldi I during a summer exercise at the Ludovika Military Academy in 1942, with white L25 tactical markings. L stands for Ludovika. The Ludovika Academy in Budapest was Hungary's official cadet training institution before 1945.

- Main armament: 40 mm 36M cannon with 50 projectiles
- Secondary armament: 7.92 mm Solothurn MG 34 machine gun with 2,000 bullets
- Engine: Manfred Weiss V-8 with 160 hp
- Maximum speed on the road: 47 km/h
- Autonomy: 200 kilometres
- Fording capacity: 0.8 metres
- Vertical obstacle clearance: 0.7 metres
- Total production: about 110 units

Toldi III (also called IIb):

- Weight: 11 tonnes
- Length: 4.95 metres
- Width: 2.06 metres
- Height: 1.85 metres
- Crew: 3 members (commander, pilot and gunner)
- Armouring: 6-43 mm
- Main armament: 40 mm 40/43M cannon with 50 projectiles
- Secondary armament: 7.92 mm Solothurn MG 34 machine gun with 2,000 bullets
- Engine: Manfred Weiss V-8 with 260 hp
- Maximum speed on the road: 60 km/h
- Autonomy: 240 kilometres
- Fording capacity: 0.9 metres
- Vertical obstacle clearance: 0.8 metres
- Total production: about 110 units.

▲ Toldi I tank with weapons not yet installed (possibly for ambulance use), 1940.

TOLDI I LIGHT TANK IN RUSSIA, 1942

▲ Toldi I 11th Reconnaissance TB, belonging to the 2nd Motorised Brigade. Note the reserve fuel serbatioi on the rear of the tank. 1942.

During its operational life, the Toldi chassis was also used for some special variants, among them, the ambulance transport and the anti-tank hunter.

Ambulance transport version (43M Toldi or Toldi eü20): Between 1942 and 1944 a limited number of Toldi tanks were modified by Ganz for use as ambulance vehicles. These modifications included increasing the size of the right turret doors and applying a red cross painted on the turret sides for identification. Initially, these vehicles were used as troop transports, but due to their limited capabilities, they were later converted into mobile ambulances to help evacuate wounded tank men during combat.

Tank destroyer (Toldi *páncélvadász*): in order to increase the firepower of the Toldi tanks, an interesting modified prototype was made that served as an anti-tank vehicle. This version, known as the 'Toldi *páncélvadász*' or 'Toldi tank destroyer', was equipped with the German Pak 40 7.5-cm anti-tank gun. However, due to Hungary's limited production capacities, only one prototype (perhaps two) of this anti-tank vehicle was made. In addition, the chassis was not able to support the additional weight when traversing rough terrain, so the project was eventually abandoned. The basis of this project by the Hungarian firm Ganz was a comparative study with the German Marder. The Hungarian model was named H-376. The use of the German gun was a test, as the Hungarian designers had not decided which gun would be mounted on the Toldi *páncélvadász in the* event of mass production. The choice would be influenced by the availability of appropriate guns and ammunition.

This Hungarian tank fighter based on the Toldi was also equipped with a Solothurn 31M light machine gun, to be used for self-defence against enemy infantry and aerial targets. Its mounting position was on the inner right side of the superstructure. At the rear of the vehicle was a large closed metal box designed to balance the weight of the main armament, which was large and heavy. This box contained some, but not all, of the ammunition and was tilted vertically to allow quick access to the 75mm rounds carried, as well as to allow the crew access to the engine underneath.

On the whole, the Toldi *páncélvadász* closely resembled the German Marder II, however, the Hungarian prototype had slightly less armour in exchange for a better power-to-weight ratio, which ensured greater mobility and a higher top speed than its German counterpart.

▲ Toldi I column and a *Csaba* military vehicle in Ukraine (USSR), 1941.

TOLDI I LIGHT TANK IN RUSSIA, 1942

▲ Toldi I painted in the typical white camouflage colour suitable for the Soviet steppe winter, 1942.

▲ View of the Hungarian Toldi tank from above.

OPERATIONAL USE

From 1940, the year of their substantial entry into service, the 38M Toldi light tanks were used in several areas, including Transylvania, Yugoslavia and Ukraine. Their real baptism of fire took place in the Ukraine in 1941, where it became evident that the mobility and manoeuvrability of the 38M Toldi tanks were superior, but their weapons and protection were inferior to other enemy vehicles encountered on the battlefield. The Toldi I tankn all its variants was present in all war events involving Hungary until 1945.

FIRST ACTION: TRANSYLVANIA CAMPAIGN

Transylvania: Transylvania was the first operation in which the Toldi was deployed, which took place in September 1940. For Hungary, the loss of Transylvania as a result of the Treaty of Trianon was a severe blow, considering its size, population and resources. This territory, after the First World War, which saw Austro-Hungary defeated, was assigned to Romania, and this loss was a constant source of irritation for the Hungarians, as the return of Transylvania to Hungary was considered a vital issue.

SECOND ACTION: JUGOSLAVIA CAMPAIGN

Occupation of Yugoslavia: the Hungarian government officially joined the Axis forces on 27 September 1940. The first joint military operation with the Axis Allies was the occupation of the Kingdom of Yugoslavia. For this operation, the Hungarian Army mobilised its Fast Corps (Gyorshadtest), consisting of the 1st and 2nd Motorised Brigades together with the 2nd Cavalry Brigade. Each of these units had one Toldi Company with 18 vehicles, for a total of 54 tanks. The 1st Cavalry Brigade was part of the Fast Corps, but was not deployed during that war.

▲ The crew of a Toldi I during a short break at the front, Russia 1941.

The first real combat use of the Toldi came during the brief April War, which was the occupation of the Kingdom of Yugoslavia by Axis forces and lasted from 6 to 17 April 1941. During this brief campaign, many Toldi tanks remained unused, mainly due to engine problems.

THIRD ACTION: ATTACK ON RUSSIA

Soviet Union: Hungary entered the war with the Soviet Union reluctantly and did not participate in the initial invasion on 22 June 1941 during the famous Operation Barbarossa. However, a Soviet preemptive air attack on Hungarian border towns on 26 June served as a pretext to declare war on 27 June. The operation initially involved the same three Celere Corps brigades that had been deployed in Yugoslavia and included 60 Ansaldo *tankettes* and 81 Toldi light tanks.

During the invasion of the Soviet Union, Hungary deployed the 1st and 2nd Motorised Brigades and the 2nd Cavalry Brigade with a total of 81 Toldi tanks. However, due to the lack of sufficient Toldi tanks, about 60

▲ A Toldi I fording a river during the invasion of Russia, 1941.

TOLDI I LIGHT TANK IN RUSSIA, 1943

▲ Toldi I bearing another well-known Hungarian armour insignia, 1943.

tankettes (L3 fast-light tanks) purchased from Italy were used to supplement the three brigades.
On 13 July 1941, the 9th Tank Battalion of the 1st Motorised Brigade attacked Soviet positions in the hills near Khmelnytskyi. During the battle, a Toldi belonging to Captain Tibor Karparthy was hit by a Soviet anti-tank gun, rendering the vehicle immobile and causing the death of the two crew members, while Captain Tibor was wounded. A second Toldi tank commanded by Sergeant Pal Habel positioned itself in front of the captain's damaged vehicle to protect it. However, this again attracted the attention of the Soviet anti-tank guns, which took Sergeant Pal's tank as a new target. The result was the loss of the tank and its crew, but this action still had the merit of saving the life of the wounded Captain Tibor. In the following Hungarian attack, the Hungarian forces managed to take the hill, destroying the three Soviet anti-tank guns. Towards the end of July 1941, the 1st Hungarian Motorised Brigade managed to destroy some 24 Soviet armoured vehicles.
Despite their initial successes, the losses of the Toldi began to increase, mainly due to mechanical failures. For this reason, these vehicles began to be mainly used for reconnaissance and infantry support due to their relatively light armour and armament.
In July 1941, due to increasing losses, Hungary was forced to send 14 more Toldi tanks to the Eastern Front, along with spare parts and engines. By August, there were a total of 57 Toldi operational on that front.
From 15 July to 8 August 1941, Hungarian forces, together with the German, Romanian and Slovakian armies, participated in the great battle of Uman, the first major victory of Operation Barbarossa!
By late October 1941, Hungarian forces had advanced almost 1,000 km into Soviet territory, reaching the Donets River. However, resupplying and reinforcing these units became increasingly difficult and complicated, with mounting casualties and the urgent need for repairs, so the Hungarians ordered the withdrawal of these forces to their homeland for recuperation and rearming.
In all these operations, the Toldi was often used for reconnaissance tasks due to its speed and agility. Its ability to move quickly across the battlefield allowed the crew to gather information on enemy positions,

▲ Toldi I tankII 1943 (note the long 40mm cannon).

TOLDI I TANKI OR III LIGHT TANK IN RUSSIA, 1943

▲ Toldi IIa or III with typical experimental reinforcements developed by Mavag. The manufacturer of the Toldi, 1943.

TOLDI I TANKII LIGHT TANK IN RUSSIA, 1943

identify weak points and transmit data to higher commands. In addition, its small size and low profile made the Toldi suitable for infiltrating and operating in areas difficult for larger vehicles to reach.
The Toldi tank also performed infantry support tasks. Its presence on the battlefield provided covering fire for troops engaged in offensive or defensive actions. Its armament of a 20 mm cannon and a 7.92 mm machine gun was effective against enemy troops, light vehicles and smaller armoured vehicles. However, the Toldi always found itself in serious difficulty when confronted with heavier enemy tanks such as the famous Soviet T-34. The Toldi's relatively light armour and modest armament made it vulnerable to attacks from more powerful enemy tanks. Therefore, the Toldi often preferred to avoid direct confrontations with enemy tanks and concentrate on reconnaissance, surveillance and tactical support missions.
The losses of the Hungarian tanks were therefore always significant, with the loss of all Italian *tankettes* and almost 80 per cent of the deployed Toldi. However, it should be noted that only 25 were damaged/lost in combat, while a larger number of 62 were lost due to mechanical failure. Most of these vehicles could be recovered, but took time to repair. As a result, only a limited number of Toldi tanks were still available for the 1942 campaign. The fighting in 1941 also highlighted the shortcomings of the Toldi, especially in terms of armament and armour. The Toldi's main gun had some chance against the less protected Soviet models of the time, but proved totally ineffective against tanks such as the T-34 and the KV series. While as repeatedly mentioned, the Toldi's armour was insufficient and could be easily penetrated by any Soviet anti-tank weapon, including anti-tank guns used by enemy infantry.
In 1942, the 1st Armoured Division was formed, using mainly T-38 tanks (Panzer 38(t) supplied by Germany), with a limited number of Toldi tanks for cover. Some 14 Toldi were assigned to the 1st Armoured

▲ A Toldi I on the march in the Hungarian countryside, note the defensive support offered to the tank leader by the open turret bore.

Reconnaissance Battalion and 5 vehicles to the 51st Anti-tank Battalion, but in reality only 17 were fully operational. By the end of August 1942, the Toldi units suffered losses and only 5 of them still remained operational. 1942 proved to be a disastrous year for the Axis forces on the Eastern Front, and a further 11 Toldi tanks were lost, if not more, depending on the source.

Siege of Stalingrad: Hungarian Toldi tanks were also present during the siege of Stalingrad, which lasted from 1942 to 1943. They operated on the outskirts of the city and were often involved in urban warfare clashes against Soviet forces.
In the summer of 1942, Hungarian Toldi tanks took part in the Battle of Voronezh, where German and Hungarian forces launched a major offensive against Soviet positions.
On this occasion, too, the Toldi tanks provided armoured support and clashed with Soviet tanks. Since 1943, due to heavy losses of equipment and men, Hungary did not send any new armoured units to the Soviet Union. In 1944, some 176 Toldi light tanks of all types were still operational (a sign that many were recovered from the damaged ones).
At that time, the frontline units using them were the 2nd Armoured Division in Galicia and the 1st Cavalry Division engaged in fighting near Warsaw. In June 1944, some 66 Toldi I and II and 63 Toldi IIa were still operational.
Unsurprisingly, even the Toldi IIa, and Toldi III, despite the addition of a cannon, were by this time completely inadequate compared to the increasingly modern armoured vehicles of the Red Army. Finally, it should be noted that after having achieved excellent results in battle with the five Marder II fighters supplied by the German ally, an equivalent fighter based on the Toldi was developed in the winter of 1944, equipped with a 7.5-cm anti-tank gun made from a decommissioned Marder. However, as already mentioned, due to limited production capacity and lack of time, no more than a single prototype was built.
After the war, the Toldi remained in operation for some time until they were replaced by Soviet equipment, as Hungary had in the meantime fallen under the Soviet Union.
Few examples of this glorious light tank are preserved today. A Toldi I and a Toldi IIa can be admired in the Kubinka Military Museum in Russia, another example is preserved in Hungary.

▲ Better than a hundred words, this shot shows just how thin the armour of the Toldi tank was!

TOLDI I LIGHT TANK IN POLAND, 1944

▲ Toldi I on the Polish front in 1944.

▲ Toldi I tank in 1943 (note the typical radio antenna bent into a circle).

▼ Toldi I tank in a barrack in Budapest 1943 (author's coloriage).

TOLDI I TANKIA LIGHT TANK IN THE CARPATHIANS, 1944

DATA SHEET			
	Toldi I	**Toldi IIa**	**Toldi III**
Length	4550 mm	4720 mm	4950 mm
Width	2060 mm	2060 mm	2060 mm
Height	1850 mm	1850 mm	1850 mm
Minimum hull height above ground	0,38 m	0,38 m	0,38 m
Weight in combat order	8.300 kg	9.500 kg	11.000 kg
Crew	3 (commander, pilot, gunner/cannoneer)		
Engine	Büssing-NAG L8V/36TR 8-cylinder, petrol-powered		
Maximum speed	43 km/h on road 30 km/h off road	47 km/h on road 30 km/h off road	60 km/h on road 30 km/h off road
Autonomy	200 km on road	200 km on road	240 km on road
Tank capacity	253 L	253 L	260 L
Armour thickness	From 6 to 35 mm	From 6 to 35 mm	From 6 to 43 mm
Armament	1 36M 20 mm cannon (Solothurn anti-tank) 1 Gebauer 34/37M 8 mm machine gun	1 L/43da 40M cannon 1 Gebauer 34/37M 8 mm machine gun	1 L/48mm 40M cannon 1 Gebauer 34/37M 8 mm machine gun
Fording capacity	0,8 m	0,8 m	0,9 m
Total production	80	110	12

▲ View of the two Toldi tanks preserved at the Russian museum in Kubinka. Wikipedia.

TOLDI I TANKN FIGHTER VERSION, 1943

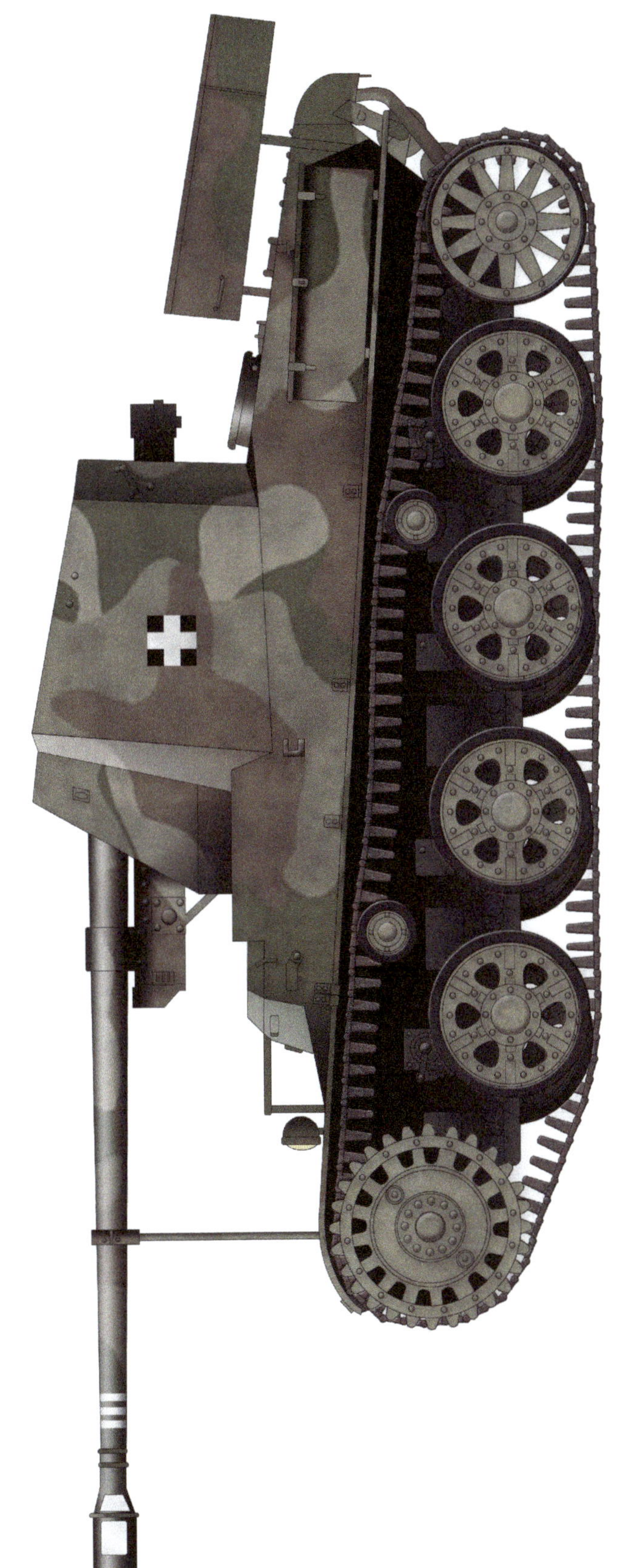

▲ Toldi fighter version, built in only one prototype (or perhaps two) and named *páncélvadász*. 1943.

▲ A Turán tank of the 2nd TB engaged in fording a river in Poland in 1944.

M40 TURÁN TANK

INTRODUCTION

After the considerable initial success of the Toldi model in the early years, it became evident that a more imposing tank would have to be developed for the future. For this reason, Hungary set out to find a medium-class armoured vehicle suitable for its armed forces.

At the beginning of 1939, shortly before German annexation, the Czech company Skoda, which had a solid reputation for weapons and tanks, proposed the revolutionary T-21 tank to Hungary. After successfully passing a series of tests, Hungary decided to acquire the production licence for the T-21 in 1940 and started local manufacture of the tank, naming it 40M Turán *közepes harckocsi* (40M Turán medium tank, or Turán I), taking its inspiration from the name of the ancient Asian homeland of the Magyar people, as recounted in the Hungarian national legend. Ultimately, Hungary sought its own tank production, based on a Czechoslovak model purchased from Germany. This model was the Turán, the Hungarian tank par excellence.

DEVELOPMENT AND DESIGN

The series production of the new 40M Turán tank was assigned to four of Hungary's leading industrial powers: Manfréd Weiss, MÁVAG, Ganz Works and Rába (referred to as MVG or Magyar Vagon in some sources), immediately after the final prototypes were considered as finalised. These well-known Hungarian metallurgical, automotive and railway companies were given an order as early as September or

▲ Turán tanks in the Royal Hungarian Army repair shop in Mátyásföld.

October 1941 for the production of 190 vehicles. The order was later increased to 230 vehicles due to production delays, and the distribution among manufacturers was that 70 were to be produced by Manfréd Weiss, 70 by Rába, 50 by Ganz and 40 by MÁVAG.
Ganz and MÁVAG received a later deadline and reduced production targets for the Turán, as they were still engaged in the production of the Toldi. In 1942, 215 more Turán were ordered as part of the Huba III plan, but the order was reduced to only 125 vehicles. In the end, only 55 of these vehicles were actually produced due to the priority given to the production of the Zrinyi assault guns based in turn on the Turán and Turán II, as stipulated in the Szabolcz Plan. In total, 285 Turán were produced.
The first delivery to the Hungarian armoured units took place in 1942, one year after the start of production and at least four years after the initial request for a medium tank, thus with a considerable delay. Sources vary on the exact number of vehicles delivered and the date, but it is generally agreed that just under 250 were delivered in 1942, while further deliveries in 1943 and 1944 amounted to less than 50 vehicles. Sources do not agree on the final actual delivery of 40M Turán in 1944.
Despite the challenges in Turán's development process compared to other countries at the time, the result was actually not as bad as it might seem at first glance. Hungary was an impoverished country with few resources, struggling to recover from a devastating war. With a weak industry, affected by the global economic depression and with little experience in tank production, several respectable tank designs were made that were modified, tested and produced in-house.
Testing began on 22 July 1941, but soon revealed serious engine problems, which is why testing was interrupted until the end of September, when repairs to the engine were carried out. Between October and December, the Turán prototype travelled 6,000 km in mountainous areas under the guidance of Colonel Tchaikovsky Emanuel. During these tests, other obvious problems with the design emerged, such as an engine cooling system that was too weak to keep the engine at a safe operating temperature unless operating in extremely cold conditions.

▲ Interesting picture of the Czechoslovakian-produced škoda T-21 prototype tank.

Other mechanical problems encountered included the risk of clogged pneumatic system hoses and the vehicle tending to get stuck in the mud. In addition, the use of the double clutch in the transmission also proved to be very problematic for the operators. However, thanks to almost 40 modifications made to the vehicle by a design office led by Erno Kovacshazy, all these mechanical problems were eventually solved. The modifications were completed in March 1942. Two months later, in May, Weiss Manfréd delivered the first four Turán with the new cooling system for crew training. It was expected that new problems would emerge during training, but in reality no significant ones were encountered. As in the first tests, the clutches continued to be difficult for the pilots to use, but there was little that could be done to solve the problem other than to continue with the training.

As the Turán represented the most complex and ambitious tank ever to enter service in Hungary, these problems were normal. During this period, the thickness of the front armour was increased to 50 mm. The weight increased to 18.2 tonnes and some final modifications were made to the engine to allow a power output of 260 hp.

During the lengthy development period of the Turán I, it became evident that in many respects the vehicle was already obsolete and unsuitable for modern combat, and so a version armed with a 75 mm cannon was developed, called the 41M Turán II. Due to the long development phase, both vehicles entered service and participated in combat at the same time.

▲ View of the Hungarian Turán tank in front.

TECHNICAL FEATURES

Hull and turret: the layout of the 40M Turán conformed to the tank standards of the time. The rear part of the hull contained the engine and transmission, while the front part housed the fighting compartment. The engine compartment could also accommodate the main fuel tanks and radiators due to the compact size of the engine. On the outside of the engine compartment were several intake grilles for engine cooling and various mounting points.

On the sides of the engine compartment were housings for tools needed to maintain and repair the vehicle and tow cables, while in the rear were two spare wheels and five smoke grenades. Used correctly, these grenades could create a smoke screen 20 metres long, 40 metres wide and 80 metres high.

The combat compartment was separated from the engine compartment by an 8 mm bulkhead and an auxiliary tank. At the front of the fighting compartment were two of the five crew members of the tank, with the pilot sitting on the right side facing a complex system of levers and pedals, and the second pilot/machinist sitting to his left. The other three crew members, namely the gunner, loader and commander, were in the three-man turret.

The gunner occupied the left side of the turret, with the loader to his right and the commander behind both, under the dome towards the rear. Each crew member had his own periscope to observe the exterior. The turret had four lifting hooks mounted on the outer corners, allowing it to be removed from the tank if necessary. Inside the turret were ammunition, a medical kit and an R5/A radio, although some ammunition was stored in the hull. The upper part of the turret also included a small hole, similar to a gun port, through which signal flags could be hoisted. Antennas for radio communications were located on the hull next to the pilot's station and at the rear of the turret.

Armament: the main cannon of the Turán was a 40 mm L/51 41M cannon. This cannon had a muzzle velocity of 812 m/s and came with 101 projectiles, which could also be used by the Nimród/SPAAG tank destroyer and later models of the Toldi light tank. The bullets available included armour-piercing and high-explosive 36M ammunition, as well as Kerngranate 42M bullets, a rocket-propelled grenade that was inserted at the end of the barrel like a large rifle grenade. However, there are no photos showing the use of a Kerngranate by a Turán, so it is possible that no Turán actually used such ammunition. At a distance of 100 metres and an angle of 60 degrees, the Turán's cannon was capable of penetrating 46 mm of armour, which decreased to 30 mm at a distance of 1,000 metres. The cannon's performance was thus slightly inferior to that of a Panzer III Ausf. H. To defend itself against infantry and unarmoured vehicles, the Turán was equipped with two 8 mm 34/40M machine guns, supplied with 3,000 rounds stored in 30 belts of 100 rounds.

Armour: the armour consisted of steel plates riveted onto a thinner inner frame. The front of the vehicle had thicker armour, 50 mm thick, obtained by riveting two thinner plates together. The outer plate was usually 35 mm thick, although in some cases 25 mm plates were used. This type of armour was only present on the almost vertical plate at the front of the fighting compartment and on the turret. The sides and rear of the hull and turret had 25 mm thick armour, while the floor and roof of the vehicle were only 13 mm thick. By the standards of the time, the Turán did not have particularly strong armour, but this was not surprising considering Hungary's limited economic and industrial resources during that period. In 1944, all Turán tanks were equipped with side skirts (also known as 'aprons' in some sources) with spaced armour similar to the German *Schürzen*. These spaced armoured skirts consisted of perforated steel plates with a thickness of 5 and 8 mm, mounted at a distance of 250 mm from the vehicle to protect it from anti-tank guns like the Soviet PTRS and PTRD. The skirts could be easily installed in the field and the necessary kits were supplied to the crews to enable installation without calling the Turán back to the workshop. Four plates were to be placed on each side of the hull and two on each side of the turret. In addition, one additional plate was placed on the rear of the turret and two on each side of the dome. The addition of the side skirts increased the overall weight of the vehicle by approximately 1 tonne.

▲ View of the Hungarian Turán tank from above.

Engine: The 40M Turán tank was equipped with a 260 hp Manfréd Weiss Z engine. This petrol engine was a V8 with a displacement of 14.866 litres and was designed to be extremely compact, allowing for a larger fuel tank. The V configuration of the engine was only 45 degrees instead of the standard 90 degree angle. This arrangement of the cylinder angles mainly influenced the sound of the engine, but had no significant impact on performance.

The liquid-cooled cast-iron engine was considered quite efficient for the time and consumed around 260 grams of petrol and 3 kg of oil per horsepower.

With a total fuel capacity of 265 litres, the tank had a range of about 165 kilometres or about 5 hours of continuous operation. The engine's ignition system featured two Bosch ignition magnets, one on each cylinder block, and ignition was battery-powered to ensure reliable operation.

However, in extremely cold conditions (below -20°C), the electric starter could malfunction, necessitating the use of a crank to start the engine. The engine's cylinders were equipped with two spark plugs each, which ensured greater reliability and, to some extent, improved performance.

The narrow angle arrangement of the engine's cylinders caused some challenges for the engineers, particularly with regard to the tight pipe bends that increased flow losses and the difficulty of installing some of the larger components due to the restricted space.

The engine was coupled to an air clutch transmission with 6 forward and reverse gears. The different speeds were achieved via two sets of planetary gears. Thanks to this system, the clutch only had to be used for the initial gear when starting and for shifting from third to fourth gear when driving.

An interesting advantage of this transmission system was the possibility of changing gears even under load. During tests conducted in 1942, the 40M Turán tank proved to be better suited to hilly terrain than the Panzerkampfwagen IV Ausf. F1, thanks to its ability to change gears on hills.

▲ Turán tank in the courtyard of the Royal Hungarian Army garage in the Mátyásföld district of Budapest.

TURÁN II TANK IN RUSSIA, 1944

▲ Turán II of the 2nd Division in 1944.

▲▼ Turán tanks in the Royal Hungarian Army repair shop in Mátyásföld (Budapest).

TURÁN TANK I IN GALICIA, 1944

Turán I of the 4th Company of the 2nd Armoured Battalion in Galicia, 1944.

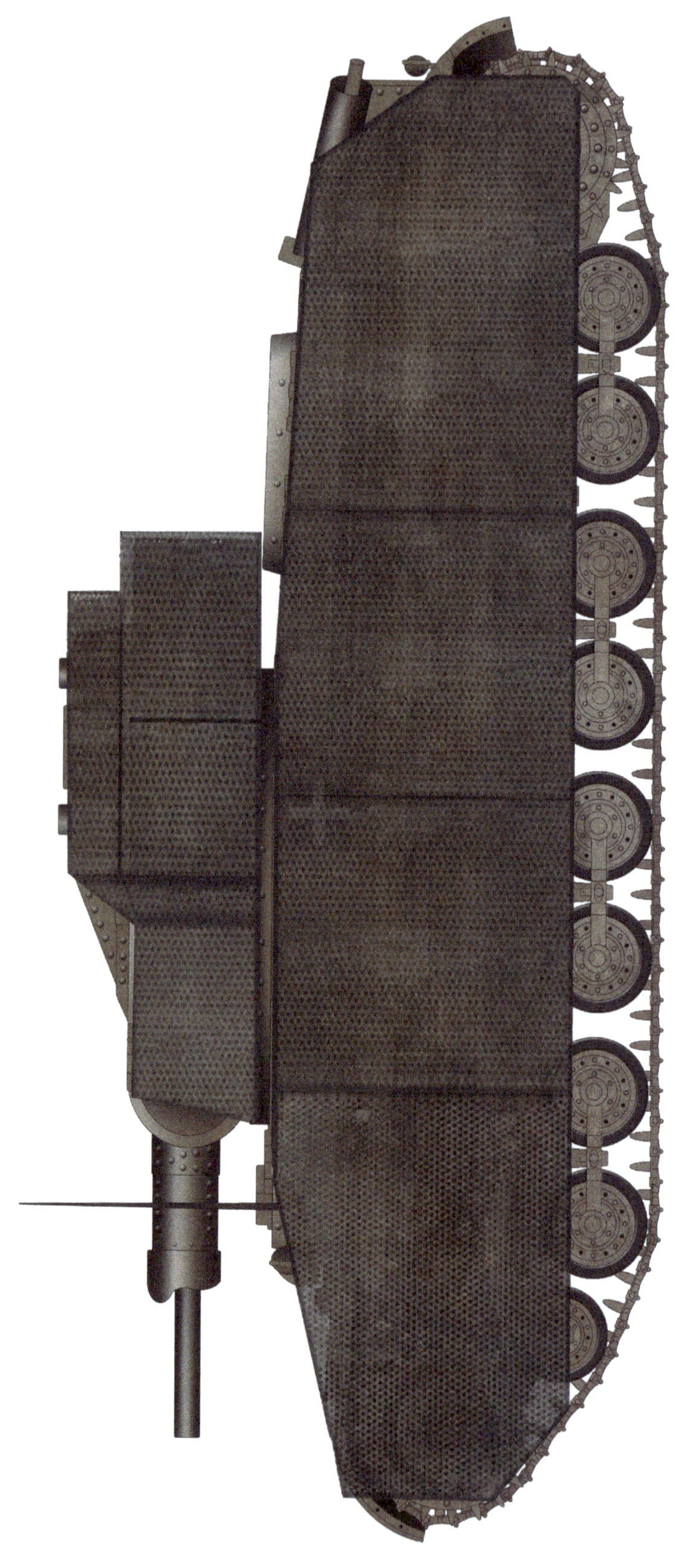

TURÁN II TANK WITH ARMOURED SKIRTS, 1944

Suspension: The bogie configuration of the Turán was largely similar to that of the LT vz.35, as it was, in fact, an evolution of that model. The suspension consisted of two bogies connected by a long bar on each side of the vehicle. Each bogie used a leaf spring consisting of 15 sheets, which supported two pivot arms, each of which supported a half bogie. Each half bogie had two pairs of rubber-rimmed road wheels, making a total of 16 individual road wheels on each side of the vehicle.

Like the LT vz.35, the Turán also had a pair of additional wheels, similar in size to road wheels, raised off the ground in front of the main suspension unit. These wheels had an aluminium rather than rubber covering, and some sources suggest that they were even sprung. These additional wheels were used to tension the tracks and tackle steep or vertical obstacles.

Above and in front of these wheels was the traction cog wheel. Most vehicles used a wheel rather than a sprocket as the traction cogwheel, but the teeth of the sprocket could help keep the treads on the bogies. Behind the traction cogwheel, in line with it, were five return rollers. Behind the fifth roller and immediately in front of the drive wheel, there was a kind of small paddle that prevented mud from accumulating on the drive wheel.

The entire rolling system consisted of 106 or 107 individual links to support the tank. Each link was 42 cm wide and applied a pressure of approximately 0.59 kg per square centimetre on the ground.

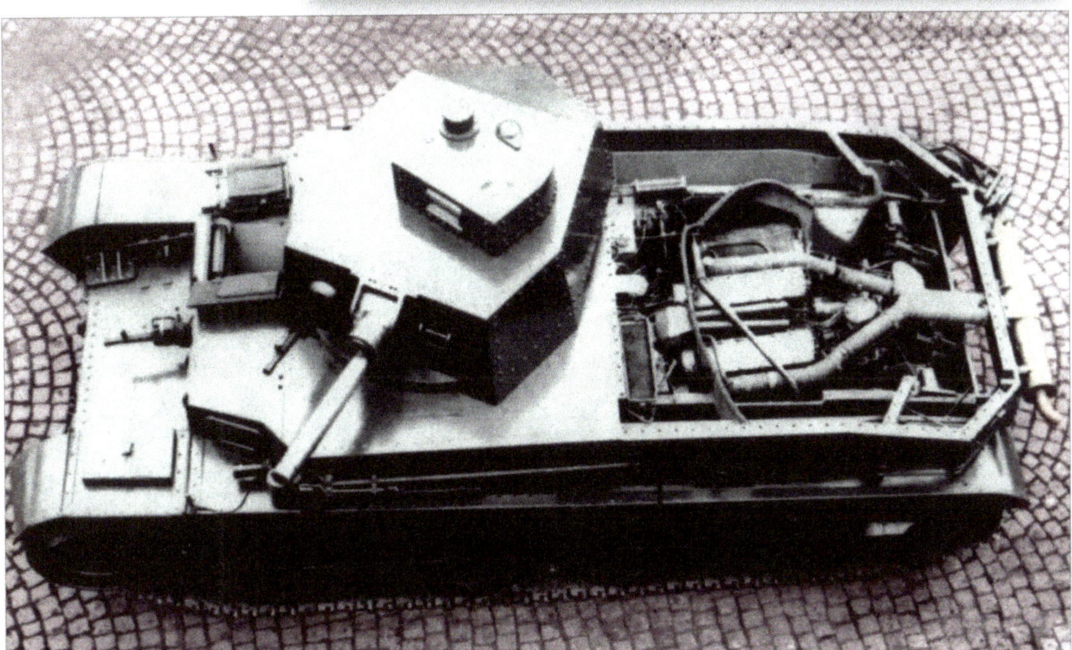

▲ Turán tank seen from above with the engine compartment open. Above a Turán tank in the Russian campaign.

▲ Turán tanks in the Royal Hungarian Army repair factory in Mátyásföld (Budapest). Above small photo: a Turán tank version II.

▼ Rückzug, Eastern Front. A Turán tank 'filled' with Hungarian soldiers. Bundesarchiv.

VERSIONS OF THE VEHICLE

Main variants:

1. **Turán I:**
   - Weight: 18 tonnes
   - Crew: 5 members (commander, gunner, loader, pilot, gunner)
   - Armouring: Front - 25 mm, Side - 15 mm, Rear - 15 mm
   - Main armament: 40 mm 40M Turán cannon
   - Secondary armament: 2 x 7.92 mm machine guns
   - Engine: Manfred Weiss petrol engine, 260 hp
   - Maximum speed on the road: 47 km/h
   - Autonomy: 200 km
2. **Turán II:**
   - Weight: 20 tonnes
   - Crew: 5 members
   - Armouring: Front - 60 mm, Side - 50 mm, Rear - 30 mm
   - Main armament: 75 mm 41M Turán cannon
   - Secondary armament: 2 x 7.92 mm machine guns
   - Engine: Manfred Weiss petrol engine, 260 hp
   - Maximum speed on the road: 47 km/h
   - Autonomy: 200 km
3. **Turán III:**
   - Weight: 21 tonnes
   - Crew: 5 members
   - Armouring: Front - 75 mm, Side - 50 mm, Rear - 40 mm
   - Main armament: 75 mm 43M Turán cannon
   - Secondary armament: 2 x 7.92 mm machine guns
   - Engine: Manfred Weiss petrol engine, 260 hp
   - Maximum speed on the road: 47 km/h
   - Autonomy: 200 km

Features common to all variants:

- Configuration: Medium tank
- Traction: Tracks
- Suspension: Ballester-Molina
- Length: approx. 5.5 metres
- Width: approx. 2.4 metres
- Height: approx. 2.7 metres
- Maximum speed over rough terrain: 20-25 km/h
- Fording capacity: 1.2 metres
- Communication system: Radio R-5
- Vision system: periscopes and loopholes for the commander and pilot

It should be noted that the technical characteristics may vary slightly between the different variants of the Turán, particularly with regard to armour and armament. This information refers to the general specifications of the main variants of the Turán tank.

41M Turán II tank: upgrading the main armament of the Turán tank had soon become a priority in order to improve its combat capabilities, as the 40 mm cannon of the initial **40 M Turán I** proved insufficient to deal effectively with the tanks of the time.
The solution adopted was to replace the 40 mm cannon with a more powerful 75 mm cannon. The cannon chosen was the 41M L/25 75 mm cannon, manufactured by MÁVAG, which was based on Bohler's 76.5 mm 18M field gun. This larger cannon required additional space in the already cramped turret of the Turán I, which eventually led to the creation of a new, larger turret for the next model, the Turán II. Although the Turán had the characteristics of a medium tank by the standards of many other countries during World War II, it was not classified as such in Hungary due to the lack of heavy armour and a tank classification system based on armament calibre. This reflected, as always, Hungary's economic and industrial limitations during that period.

43M Turán III tank Again in early 1943 and almost simultaneously with the design of the Turán II, the General Staff ordered a heavy tank equipped with the German-supplied KwK 40 L/43, in order to have a truly effective vehicle in the field; the piece was modified by the Hungarians to fire both German ammunition and special grenades of their own design. Only one prototype was built, called the *hasszu nehez harckocsi* ('long heavy tank') and later '43M Turán III': equipped with thicker armour, it had an even wider turret, with a retracted and raised dome that gave it a distinctive profile. Otherwise it remained identical to the Turán II. The vehicle was never mass-produced and was destroyed at an unspecified time during the invasion of Hungary.

VEHICLES DERIVED FROM TURÁN

44M Zrinyi I and 43M Zrinyi II assault guns**:** the Zrinyi assault guns of Hungary were similar to the German StuG III. These vehicles took the enlarged hull of the Turán tank as a basis and replaced the turret and superstructure with a low casemate. This configuration allowed a larger cannon to be mounted than could be accommodated in a standard turret, but also entailed certain limitations related to the lack of a rotating turret. The Zrinyi project included two main variants: the 44M Zrinyi I, which was equipped with a 75mm 43M long-barreled anti-tank gun developed by MÁVAG, and the 43M Zrinyi II, which was armed with a 105mm 40/43M howitzer, also produced by MÁVAG. However, due to the difficulties encountered with the 75 mm gun, only the Zrinyi II version was produced.
The Zrinyi II proved to be an effective assault cannon and represented a step forward for Hungary in its attempt to integrate a powerful cannon into a turret vehicle. The name 'Zrinyi' was chosen in honour of Miklós IV Zrinyi, a famous Hungarian and Croatian military leader and legendary hero who fought against Ottoman forces in the Siege of Szigetvár in 1566.

▲ Turán III 44M prototype.

TURÁN II TANK IN RUSSIA-POLAND, 1944

▲ Turán II of the 2nd Mechanized Division, 1944.

DATA SHEET			
	40 M Turán I	**41 M Turán II**	**43 M Turán III**
Length	5550 mm	5550 mm	5550 mm
Width	2444 mm	2444 mm	2444 mm
Height	2390 mm	2390 mm	2390 mm
Minimum hull height above ground	0,38 m	0,38 m	0,40 m
Weight in combat order	18.000 kg	20.000 kg	21.000 kg
Crew	5	5	5
Engine	Weiss Manfréd Z-V8H-4 260 hp (195 kW)		
Maximum speed	47 km/h on road	47 km/h on road	47 km/h on road
Autonomy	200 km on road 5 h off road	200 km on road 5 h off road	200 km on road 5 h off road
Tank capacity	265 L	265 L	265 L
Armour thickness	From 15 to 25 mm	From 30 to 60 mm	From 40 to 75 mm
Armament	Turán 40M 40mm cannon + 2 x 7.92mm machine guns	41M Turán 75 mm cannon + 2 x 7.92 mm machine guns	75 mm 43M Turán cannon + 2 x 7.92 mm machine guns

▲ Turán II engaged in the Battle of Torda. An L3 Ansaldo light tank leads the assault. Bundesarchiv.

OPERATIONAL USE

The first 12 mass-produced Turán were used for training purposes at the Armed Forces School in May 1942. The remaining vehicles produced were assigned to the 1st Tank Regiment, until Hungary accumulated about 30 Turán. During the summer, it became apparent that further improvements to tank transmissions were needed, so every tank was returned to the manufacturers to solve these problems. Units destined for the Eastern Front received imported vehicles as replacements.

On 17 April 1944, the Turán saw combat for the first time in Galicia, in the Polish-Ukrainian border region, with the Hungarian 2nd Armoured Division. In order to confuse the Soviets, the Hungarian vehicles had their markings smeared with mud to make them less identifiable. However, the large national cross painted on the back of the hull remained visible to allow identification by Allied aircraft.

During a clash with a small group of Soviet T-34 tanks in a wooded area with streams from melting snow, 30 Turán tanks were lost, both the 40 mm 40M and the 75 mm 41M variant. However, only two T-34/85s were destroyed, both by a Turán II 41M. These losses were significant, representing around 30 per cent of the tanks deployed by the 2nd Armoured Division. Nevertheless, the remaining tanks managed to capture the towns of Nadvirna (Nadwórna) and Deliatyn (Deliatin).

Between the beginning of June and mid-July, the 1st Cavalry Division fought against the Soviet defences along a line stretching from Luninets (Luninec) to Brest, suffering heavy material losses. In the following September, the 2nd Armoured Division employed its Turán in the capture of Turda (Torda). During the autumn, the 124 Turán of the 1st Armoured Division were employed in operations near Arad, Debrecen and Nyíregyháza, and as with the other divisions, many vehicles were lost.

The conclusions drawn by the crews using these vehicles were that the gun was simply too weak to play a valid anti-tank role against the T-34/85. Although the Turán's capabilities were inferior to those of the tanks of the time, the Germans, fighting alongside the Hungarians, recognised that it performed better than could be expected.

At least one Turán, probably belonging to the 1st Cavalry Division, was captured by Yugoslav partisans in Senta in 1944. It is not known whether this tank was later used by the partisans, and virtually all other details about it remain unknown.

It is known that at least one Turán I and one Turán II were taken to the Russian tank testing ground at Kubinka. At present, the only known Turán II is on display in the Kubinka Tank Museum, but it is not known whether a Turán I still exists hidden in storage. Outside of this remote possibility, it is believed that all other Turán I tanks were destroyed in combat or ended up as scrap heaps.

CONCLUSION

Had the 40M Turán I entered service in the 1930s, it might have proved to be a capable design. However, due to difficulties and delays in its production and introduction, the tank failed to reach its full potential when it finally entered service in 1944.

Negotiations with Italy and Germany, which provided no technical support and supplies for the project, were not always efficient and cooperative, causing further delays. These delays in the production and introduction of the 40M Turán I made the vehicle obsolete compared to the more modern tanks used by the adversaries during the Second World War.

Once in service, the 40M Turán I revealed its flaws and limitations due to its outdated design and technology. This contributed to its bad reputation as an insignificant tank, particularly when compared to the more advanced tanks used by allies and enemies.

Despite these criticisms, it is important to recognise that the 40M Turán I played an important role in the development of other Hungarian tanks and the country's heavy industry. The lessons learnt from the

▲ Two Turán IIs in their hangars. Note the raised weapon system.

▼ A Turán II with the famous protective skirts attached forms the background of this beautiful photo. Wikipedia.

design and use of the Turán I helped Hungary advance in the field of tanks and develop more modern and high-performance vehicles later on.
In conclusion, although the 40M Turán I had several flaws and a negative reputation, its contribution in the context of the development of the Hungarian tank industry and technology cannot be underestimated.

▲ A Turán II tank operating in the Russian campaign advances over the heavy steppe terrain. 1944.

► Budapest at the end of the war was the scene of particularly fierce clashes that ended the inauspicious military adventure of the Hungarians alongside the Nazi troops.

TURÁN II TANK IN HUNGARY, 1945

▲ Turán II of the 2nd Armoured Division in Budapest, Hungary, winter 1945.

TURÁN II TANK IN HUNGARY, 1945

▲ Turán II of the 2nd Armoured Division in Hungary, 1945.

BIBLIOGRAPHY

- И.П. Шмелёв, *Бронетанковая техника Венгрии (1940–1945). (etwa: I.P. Schmeljow: Gepanzerte Fahrzeuge Ungarns (1940–1945).) ExPrint Ltd., Moskau, 1995.*
- Iván T. Berend, György Ránki: *The development of the manufacturing industry in Hungary, 1900–1944. Akademiai Kaido, 1960.*
- D. Nešić, (2008), *Naoružanje Drugog Svetsko Rata-Nemačka, Beograd*
- B. Adam, E. Miklos, S. Gyula (2006) *A Magyar Királyi Honvédség külföldi gyártású páncélos harcjárművei 1920-1945, Petit Real*
- S.J.Zaloga (2013) *Tanks of Hitler's Eastern Allies 1941-45, New Vanguard.*
- N. Thomas and L. P. Szabo (2010) *The Royal Hungarian Army in World War II, Osprey.*
- A. T. Jones (2013) *Armored Warfare and Hitler's Allies 1941-1945, Pen and Sword*
- Bojan B. Dumitrijević and Dragan Savić (2011) *Oklopne jedinice na Jugoslovenskom ratištu,, Institut za savremenu istoriju, Beograd*
- G. Finizio (1987) *Hungarian Armor, Wheels and Tracks.*
- P. Chamberlain and C. Ellis (1977) *Axis Combat Vehicles, Arco Publishing Company*
- J. C. M. Probst, *Hungarian armour during World War 2: The Turán tank and its derivatives from Airfix Magazine issue 9, 1976*
- Leo W.G. Niehorster , *The Royal Hungarian Army, 1920- 1945*
- TAC News , *The Hungarians on the Eastern Front*
- Németh Károly , *Straussler Miklós Tankjai*
- Vladimír Francev & Charles K. Kliment, *Československa Obrnena Vozidla 1918-48*
- Janusz Magnuski, *Armor in Pancerne Profile 1*
- Bombay, Gyarmati & Turcsányi, *Harckocsik 1916-tól napjainkig*
- B.Attila, S Gyula, W. Laszlo, *A Magyar Kiralyi Honvedseg Fegyverzete*
- Axworthy, Mark (1995). *Third Axis, Fourth Ally: Romanian Armed Forces in the European War, 1941–1945. London: Arms and Armour. ISBN 978-1-85409-267-0.*
- Bernad, Dénes & Kliment, Charles K. (2015). *Magyar Warriors: The History of the Royal Hungarian Armed Forces, 1919–1945. Vol. 1. Solihull, UK: Helion. ISBN 978-1-906033-88-0.*
- Csaba, Becze (2007). *Magyar Steel: Hungarian Armour in WWII. Sandomierz, Poland: STRATUS for Mushroom Model Publications. ISBN 978-83-89450-29-6.*
- Kliment, Charles K. & Francev, Vladimír (1997). *Czechoslovak Armored Fighting Vehicles 1918-1948. Atlgen, Pennsylvania: Schiffer Publishing. ISBN 0-7643-0141-1.*
- Mujzer, Péter (2018). *Operational History of the Hungarian Armoured Troops in World War II. Lublin, Poland: Kagero Publications. ISBN 978-83-66148-07-9.*

ALREADY PUBLISHED BOOKS

ALL TITLES ARE PUBLISHED IN ENGLISH AND ITALIAN LANGUAGE

VISIT OUR WEBSITE FOR MORE INFORMATION ON THE WEAPONS ENCYCLOPAEDIA SERIES:

https://soldiershop.com/collane/libri/the-weapons-encyclopaedia/

TWE-013 EN

www.ingramcontent.com/pod-product-compliance
Ingram Content Group UK Ltd.
Pitfield, Milton Keynes, MK11 3LW, UK
UKHW061954290726
14090UKWH00021B/1225